ASHLEY TERRADEZ

GOD WANTS YOU RICH

The Scandalous Truth

STUDY GUIDE

God Wants You Rich Study Guide

ISBN: 978-1-7335938-5-4

Table of Contents

WELCOME...1
WEEK 1: UNDERSTANDING BIBLICAL PROSPERITY.......................5
WEEK 2: GOD'S NATURE AS PROVIDER....................................7
WEEK 3: THE PURPOSE OF PROSPERITY..................................9
WEEK 4: JESUS' WEALTH ON EARTH.......................................11
WEEK 5: JESUS' MINISTRY PROVISION....................................13
WEEK 6: JESUS BECAME POOR FOR YOU...................................15
WEEK 7: MONEY MYTHS & MINDSETS.......................................17
WEEK 8: THE LIE OF LACK...19
WEEK 9: RENEWING THE MIND...21
WEEK 10: TWO COMPETING SYSTEMS...23
WEEK 11: THE SEED SYSTEM..25
WEEK 12: SUPERNATURAL MULTIPLICATION...............................27
WEEK 13: GRACE-BASED PROSPERITY...29
WEEK 14: FAITH FOR FINANCES...31
WEEK 15: REMOVING UNBELIEF..33
WEEK 16: ROLE OF DILIGENCE..35
WEEK 17: EXCELLENCE & WORK HABITS.......................................37
WEEK 18: DILIGENCE WITHOUT STRIVING....................................39
WEEK 19: GIVING AS FAITH...41
WEEK 20: TYPES OF GIVING...43
WEEK 21: LIFESTYLE OF GENEROSITY...45
CONCLUSION...47

WELCOME

Welcome to the *God Wants You Rich 21-Week Study Guide*—a journey designed to help you discover the truth about God's heart for your provision, abundance, and financial freedom. Whether you are going through this study on your own or with a group, you are about to explore life-changing revelation rooted in the goodness of God, His covenant promises, and the finished work of Jesus.

For many believers, finances have been an area filled with confusion, fear, or religious baggage. This study is an opportunity to set all of that aside and let the Word of God speak clearly and boldly. Throughout these 21 weeks, you will renew your mind, build your faith, and gain practical understanding of how to walk in the abundance Jesus paid for.

ABOUT THIS STUDY

This guide is structured as a **21-week journey** based on the seven chapters of *God Wants You Rich*. Each chapter is divided into **three focused sessions**, allowing you to go deeper without feeling rushed and giving room for reflection, discussion, and real-life application.

Every weekly session includes:

- **Teaching Highlights** from the chapter
- **Reflection & Discussion** questions
- **Application** steps
- **A Declaration of Faith** to speak aloud
- **A Prayer** to reinforce the truth you're learning

This structure makes it ideal for:

- Personal growth
- Small groups
- Bible studies
- Discipleship groups

HOW TO USE THIS STUDY GUIDE

1. Read the chapter portion first.

Each week builds on the section of *God Wants You Rich* assigned to that session. Reading the chapter text first ensures the teaching highlights and reflections strengthen what you've already read.

2. Engage thoughtfully with the questions.

Your answers can change over time as your understanding grows. Be honest, be expectant, and allow the Lord to challenge old beliefs.

3. Let the Holy Spirit lead you.

Ask Him to highlight what He wants to show you each week. He will reveal to you what you need to know and understand.

4. Apply what you learn.

Faith is not passive. Many weeks include small, practical steps—these are opportunities to activate your faith in practical ways and experience real results.

5. Speak the declarations out loud.

Your words shape your beliefs and steer your life. Speaking truth sparks and develops transformation. Each declaration is crafted to help you agree with what God has already said about your provision.

6. Pray intentionally.

Every session ends with a suggested prayer focus. These are not formulas but conversation starters between you and your Heavenly Father.

7. Take your time.

This is not a race! These truths are meant to be absorbed, meditated on, and practiced. Give the Holy Spirit space to speak to you in each principle.

A NOTE FOR GROUP LEADERS

If you are leading a group:

- Read the week's material and the corresponding book section ahead of time.
- Encourage participation but avoid pressure.
- Keep the atmosphere full of grace, joy, and expectation.
- Allow time for testimony—this study often releases breakthrough.
- Remember: The goal is not to "get through content." The goal is **transformation**.

WHAT YOU CAN EXPECT OVER THE NEXT 21 WEEKS

By the end of this study, you will:

- Understand God's true heart for your financial prosperity
- Remove religious misconceptions that have held you back
- Learn how to operate in Kingdom economics instead of worldly systems
- Build practical habits of faith, diligence, generosity, and stewardship
- Recognize the biblical purpose of abundance
- Grow in confidence that God is your source
- Experience freedom in your financial thinking and decision-making

- Learn to live generously from a place of overflow
- See prosperity as part of Jesus' finished work

This is more than a study—it's an invitation to step into the abundant life God intended for you!

INTRODUCTION TO THE JOURNEY

The title of the book—*God Wants You Rich*—is intentionally provocative because it confronts decades of tradition, misconception, and religious discomfort. These four words have stirred controversy not because they are untrue, but because they **expose the lies** that have kept believers limited.

This study begins with the foundation that:

- God is a good Father.
- Good Fathers provide for their children.
- And God is not glorified in your lack—He is glorified in your fruitfulness.

As you progress through the next 21 weeks, expect to have long-held beliefs challenged, expectations lifted, and faith activated. Expect the Holy Spirit to reveal where scarcity mindsets have taken root and to replace them with truth. And expect to encounter the generosity of God in a fresh way.

UNDERSTANDING BIBLICAL PROSPERITY

WEEK 1

Prosperity doesn't begin with money.
It begins with God's heart.

Chapter One of *God Wants You Rich* opens by defining true prosperity from a biblical standpoint. Many believers have inherited distorted ideas about wealth—viewing money as something dangerous and evil or assuming that poverty is somehow spiritual. Scripture reveals a very different picture.

Biblical prosperity is not greed, excess, or materialism. It is **abundance with purpose**, rooted in the goodness of God. Throughout the Bible, God consistently blessed His people so they could live, give, and serve without the bondage of lack. Prosperity includes finances, but it is not limited to them—it also encompasses peace, wisdom, relationships, opportunities, and the ability to fulfill your God-given purpose.

Ashley emphasizes that God wants His children to prosper because He is a good Father. A healthy parent desires their children to have everything they need—not just to survive, but to flourish. Likewise, God's heart toward you is provision, not deprivation; increase, not insufficiency!

Understanding prosperity begins with removing religious filters and seeing wealth the way Scripture presents it: as **a blessing from a generous God**. This foundation prepares you to receive everything He has already made available in Christ.

REFLECTION & DISCUSSION

1. How would you have defined "prosperity" before reading this chapter?

2. Does it challenge you to think of God as a Father who desires your abundance? Why or why not?

3. Which beliefs about money or prosperity do you sense may have come more from tradition or fear than from Scripture?

APPLICATION | ***ACTION STEPS***

Write down one belief you have held about prosperity—positive or negative.

Now invite God to show you one area where He wants to expand your expectations this week.

RENEW YOUR MIND

Throughout the week, speak and meditate on this truth:

"God wants me to prosper because He is good."

Let this truth reshape your expectations this week.

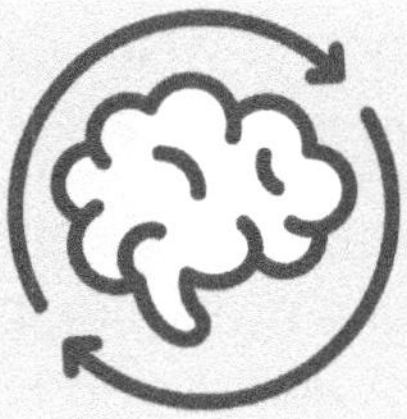

DECLARATION OF FAITH

"God is a good Father, and He delights in my prosperity.
I receive His abundance—not by striving, but by trusting Him.
My mind is being renewed, my expectations are rising,
and I am learning to see prosperity the way He does."

Prayer

Father, thank You for revealing Your true heart toward me. Help me see prosperity the way You see it—clean, holy, purposeful, and rooted in Your goodness. Remove every false belief and renew my mind as I study Your Word. I open my heart to Your abundance and choose to trust You fully. In Jesus' Name, amen.

GOD'S NATURE AS PROVIDER

WEEK 2

Provision isn't something God occasionally does. It's who He is.

One of the greatest misunderstandings in the body of Christ is the idea that God only provides in emergencies, or that His care is inconsistent, conditional, or reluctant. But Scripture reveals a completely different picture! Provision is not simply an action God performs—it's part of His very nature!

From the beginning, God revealed Himself as the One who sees ahead and provides. Before Adam and Eve had a need, God created a world overflowing with everything required for them to flourish. In the Old Testament, He revealed one of His covenant names as ***Jehovah Jireh***—"The Lord Will Provide." A name reveals character. This means provision is not merely what God does; it's who He is.

Ashley explains that when believers struggle to trust God with their needs, it is often because they haven't fully understood His heart. God is not withholding. He is generous. He is purposeful. He is abundant. **His provision reflects His goodness, not our performance.**

Learning to see God as your Provider reshapes your relationship with money. Instead of striving, fearing, or attempting to secure everything in your own strength, you begin to rest in His faithfulness. Prosperity becomes less about accumulation and more about confidence—confidence that your Father knows what you need, cares deeply for you, and delights in supplying every good thing to you!

REFLECTION & DISCUSSION

1. Do you naturally think of God as your Provider, or has that been difficult for you to believe? Why?

2. When you read the name "Jehovah Jireh," what does that reveal to you about God's character?

3. How would your daily life change if you truly believed God delights in providing for you?

APPLICATION | ***ACTION STEPS***

Write one way you've seen God provide for you in the past.

This week, look for one opportunity to trust Him in a small, practical decision. Write it down!

RENEW YOUR MIND

Throughout the week, speak and meditate on this truth:

"God is my Provider, and He is faithful."

Let this settle into your heart as you reflect on His nature.

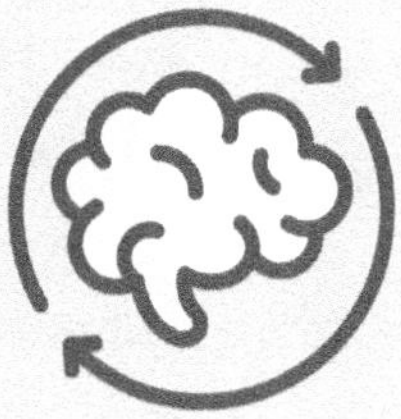

DECLARATION OF FAITH

"God is my Provider. He sees my needs and supplies them abundantly.
I trust His goodness, I rest in His care, and I rely on His faithfulness.
I refuse fear and choose confidence in His provision."

Prayer

Father, thank You for revealing Yourself as my Provider. Help me see Your goodness in every area of my life. Teach me to trust Your timing, Your wisdom, and Your generosity. I release my worries and receive Your provision with confidence and gratitude. In Jesus' Name, amen.

THE PURPOSE OF PROSPERITY

WEEK 3

When you misunderstand the purpose of something, you misuse it, and eventually distrust it.

Prosperity becomes controversial when people misunderstand its purpose. Many believers have been taught that wealth is inherently ungodly or that desire for increase is selfish. But Scripture reveals a very different perspective. God's purpose for prosperity is not materialism, indulgence, or status—it is **kingdom effectiveness, freedom, and generosity**.

Ashley explains that money itself is not the problem. The heart behind it is what matters. When prosperity is understood through the lens of God's character, it becomes a tool that empowers believers to live free from the bondage of lack and to actively participate in advancing the Gospel.

Correcting misconceptions about prosperity starts with recognizing that:

- God is not glorified by your lack.
- Poverty does not produce holiness.
- Scarcity is not spiritual maturity.

Abundance is not selfish when guided by God's purpose.

Throughout Scripture, God blessed His people so they could be a blessing, fulfill their calling, support His work, and reveal His goodness. Prosperity equips you to give, to serve, to step out boldly, and to make a real impact.

When misconceptions fall away, you gain clarity: **prosperity is not the goal—God is. Prosperity is simply part of His provision on the journey.**

REFLECTION & DISCUSSION

1. What misconceptions about prosperity did you grow up hearing or absorbing?

2. How does understanding God's purpose for prosperity change the way you think about money?

3. What fears or hesitations come up when you think about increasing financially?

APPLICATION | ***ACTION STEPS***

Write one purpose you believe God has for prospering you.

Do one simple act this week that reflects that purpose—such as helping, blessing, or encouraging someone. Document what you did.

RENEW YOUR MIND

Throughout the week, speak and meditate on this truth:

"Prosperity has a purpose in my life."

Return to this phrase whenever you need clarity and direction.

DECLARATION OF FAITH

"I reject every misconception about prosperity that does not align with God's Word.
I embrace His purpose for abundance in my life—not for selfishness, but for impact.
God's provision equips me, frees me, and empowers me to be a blessing."

Prayer

Father, thank You for revealing the true purpose of prosperity. Remove every false belief I've carried and renew my understanding according to Your Word. Teach me to use what You give for Your glory, Your kingdom, and the good of others. Help me walk in freedom, boldness, and generosity. In Jesus' Name, amen.

JESUS' WEALTH ON EARTH

WEEK 4

Jesus wasn't poor. He was purposeful.

One of the most persistent misconceptions in Christian tradition is the belief that Jesus lived in poverty. While this idea may sound humble or spiritual, it is simply not supported by Scripture. In fact, the Bible consistently reveals that Jesus operated from a place of **provision, stability, and abundance**—never lack.

Ashley shows that Jesus' life demonstrates several indicators of wealth:

- He wore a seamless tunic valuable enough for soldiers to cast lots over.
- He had ministry partners who supported Him financially.
- He traveled extensively, fed crowds, gave to the poor, and had a treasurer—even though Judas was stealing from the money bag.
- The gifts brought to Him at birth were of tremendous value and would have sustained His family for years.

Jesus was never depicted as struggling to meet His needs or unable to fulfill His mission due to financial constraints. Rather, He moved freely, generously, and confidently—fully equipped for every good work the Father called Him to do.

Understanding this truth matters, because if Jesus modeled abundant provision, then poverty cannot be considered holy. Jesus showed us what it looks like to live with **God as Source**, and that includes having what you need—and more than enough—to accomplish His purpose.

REFLECTION & DISCUSSION

1. Before this study, did you believe Jesus lived in poverty? What shaped that belief?

2. How does seeing Jesus as well-supplied affect the way you view God's will for your own provision?

3. What does Jesus' example show you about the relationship between abundance and purpose?

APPLICATION | ***ACTION STEPS***

Write down one misconception you may have held about Jesus and wealth.

Take one moment this week to thank Him specifically for being your abundant Provider.

RENEW YOUR MIND

Throughout the week, speak and meditate on this truth:

"Jesus lacked nothing, and I lack nothing in Him."

Let this truth remind you of His fullness in you!

DECLARATION OF FAITH

"Jesus modeled abundance, purpose, and provision.
I reject the myth that poverty is holy or spiritual.
I embrace the truth that God supplies what I need to fulfill my calling,
just as He supplied everything Jesus needed."

Prayer

Father, thank You for showing me the truth about Jesus' life on earth. Help me see abundance the way You see it, and remove every false belief about poverty and holiness. Teach me to trust You the same way Jesus did—with confidence, freedom, and purpose. In Jesus' Name, amen.

JESUS' MINISTRY PROVISION

WEEK 5

Jesus didn't minister from scarcity, but from supply.

Jesus' ministry was not a bare-bones, hand-to-mouth operation. Scripture reveals that He operated with consistent and abundant provision—enough to sustain a team, travel, give generously, and meet the needs of others. Far from being financially strained, Jesus functioned with resources, structure, and support that reflected God's ongoing supply.

Ashley highlights several key truths:

- **Jesus had ministry partners**—people who supported Him financially (Luke 8:1–3).
- **He had a treasurer**, which only makes sense if there was money to manage (John 12:6).
- **There was enough surplus in His ministry to give to the poor**, something His disciples assumed as a normal practice.
- **His team traveled frequently**, a costly undertaking in their time.
- **He always had what was needed**—whether feeding multitudes, hosting gatherings, or meeting urgent needs.

Even Judas, who was stealing from the ministry funds, did not create a crisis. Jesus never worried about lack, never begged for resources, and never scaled back His mission due to financial pressure. He demonstrated a life fully resourced by the Father.

This matters because misrepresenting Jesus as financially destitute creates a distorted model for Christian living. Jesus showed us what it looks like to trust God for continual provision while pursuing a God-given mission—confident, supplied, and free.

REFLECTION & DISCUSSION

1. What stands out to you most about the way Jesus' ministry was funded and supported?

2. Does it surprise you that Jesus' ministry regularly gave to the poor? Why or why not?

3. How does Jesus' example challenge the idea that ministry must be small, struggling, or underfunded?

APPLICATION | *ACTION STEPS*

Write one area where you want to grow in trusting God's practical provision.

Look for a "provision moment" this week and acknowledge it as His goodness toward you.

RENEW YOUR MIND

Throughout the week, speak and meditate on this truth:

God's provision flows to me through both supernatural and practical means."

Allow this to broaden your expectations of how God supplies.

DECLARATION OF FAITH

"God provides for the mission He gives.
Just as Jesus' ministry was supplied, mine is supplied.
I refuse to fear lack.
I trust God to fund His purpose in my life abundantly and continually."

Prayer

Father, thank You for showing me the truth about how You supplied Jesus' ministry. Help me trust You for my own calling with the same confidence. Remove fear, hesitation, and small thinking. Teach me to expect Your provision and walk boldly in what You've assigned to me. In Jesus' Name, amen.

JESUS BECAME POOR FOR YOU

WEEK 6

Jesus took your poverty so you could receive His abundance."

Understanding biblical prosperity requires looking at the cross—not just as the place where Jesus dealt with sin, sickness, and shame, but also where He dealt with **poverty itself**. Ashley explains that one of the great exchanges of redemption is found in 2 Corinthians 8:9: *"Though He was rich, yet for your sake He became poor, so that you through His poverty might become rich."*

This does not refer to Jesus living a life of earthly poverty (as Weeks 4 and 5 established). Instead, it speaks of what He took upon Himself **during His crucifixion**, when He was stripped, humiliated, forsaken, and emptied of everything—materially, socially, physically, and spiritually.

At the cross:

- Jesus bore the curse of lack.
- He experienced complete deprivation.
- He took on the effects of sin that brought scarcity into the world.
- He absorbed the consequences of Adam's fall, including toil and insufficiency.

Why? So that **you could walk in the blessing of abundance**, free from the chokehold of fear, striving, and never measuring up. Just as Jesus became sin so you could become righteous, and became a curse so you could receive the blessing, **He became poor so you could become rich**—fully supplied, fully equipped, and fully empowered to live the life God designed for you! Prosperity, then, is not selfish—it is part of your inheritance in Christ.

REFLECTION & DISCUSSION

1. How does viewing prosperity as part of Jesus' redemptive work change your perspective?

2. What does "Jesus became poor for you" mean to you personally?

3. Are there areas where you have accepted lack as normal or unavoidable? What might Jesus be inviting you to change?

APPLICATION | ***ACTION STEPS***

Write a sentence describing what it means to you that Jesus became poor so you could become rich.

Receive the truth you just wrote by speaking it aloud once each day this week. Write how you feel your mind has already begun to change regarding how you view finances.

RENEW YOUR MIND

Throughout the week, speak and meditate on this truth:

"Jesus became poor so I could become rich."

Let this truth reinforce your confidence in His finished work.

DECLARATION OF FAITH

"Jesus became poor for me so that I might walk in His richness.
Lack is not my identity, and poverty is not my inheritance.
I receive the abundance Jesus provided—freely, joyfully, and confidently."

Prayer

Father, thank You that Jesus took my poverty at the cross so I could walk in Your abundance. Help me see every area where lack has tried to shape my thinking. Renew my mind, strengthen my faith, and teach me to live boldly in the richness of Your provision. In Jesus' Name, amen.

MONEY MYTHS & MINDSETS

WEEK 7

A wrong belief can limit your life just as much as a lack of money.

Many Christians struggle financially not because God is withholding from them, but because their **mindsets** have been shaped by tradition, fear, or misinformation rather than Scripture. Ashley explains that the enemy doesn't need to steal your money if he can steal your faith—because a wrong belief will keep you from receiving what God has already provided.

Common money myths include:

- "Money is evil."
- "God uses poverty to teach lessons."
- "It's more spiritual to have less."
- "You shouldn't expect God to bless you financially."
- "Prosperity is selfish."
- "Rich Christians must be greedy."

These ideas are deeply rooted in religious culture, not the Bible. In Scripture, God consistently blessed His people—not to inflate their egos, but to empower their purpose.

Wrong thinking creates internal resistance. Even when people believe God can bless them, money myths make them doubt whether He **wants to**. These mindsets produce guilt around abundance, fear around giving, and hesitation in believing God for more.

Renewing your mind means identifying the lies you've believed and replacing them with truth. When your beliefs align with God's Word, faith becomes natural—and prosperity becomes possible!

REFLECTION & DISCUSSION

1. Which money myth have you encountered most often in church or culture?

2. Have you ever felt guilty or hesitant about wanting financial increase? Why?

3. What new mindset is God inviting you to adopt regarding money?

APPLICATION | *ACTION STEPS*

Identify one money myth you've believed in the past.

Then replace it by choosing one simple truth from Scripture or this chapter's teaching you will consciously focus on whenever that lie tries to rise.

RENEW YOUR MIND

Throughout the week, speak and meditate on this truth:

"I reject lies and embrace God's truth about money."

Use this phrase to redirect your thoughts whenever old mindsets surface.

DECLARATION OF FAITH

"I reject every money myth and every belief that does not reflect God's Word.
My mind is being renewed, my faith is growing,
and I choose truth over tradition.
God's abundance is His will for me."

Prayer

Father, thank You for revealing the truth about money and renewing my thinking. Show me every belief that has limited me and replace it with Your Word. I receive clarity, freedom, and confidence as You reshape my mindset. In Jesus' Name, amen.

THE LIE OF LACK

WEEK 8

Lack is not just a circumstance—it's a strategy.

Lack often appears natural, inevitable, and circumstantial—but Scripture reveals that it is one of the enemy's primary strategies to limit believers. Ashley explains that the enemy does not need to destroy your calling if he can convince you that you **don't have enough** to fulfill it.

Lack-based thinking shows up in thoughts like:

- "I can't afford to obey God."
- "I don't have enough to give."
- "My future is uncertain because my resources are limited."
- "Once things improve financially, then I'll pursue what God has told me."

These thoughts are designed to delay obedience, weaken confidence, and create dependency on the world's system. The enemy uses lack to produce fear—fear of stepping out, fear of generosity, fear of making mistakes, fear of trusting God.

In Scripture, every instance of God calling someone to do something significant required **faith beyond natural resources**. God asked Moses to lead a nation without a strategy, Gideon to defeat an army without manpower, and the disciples to feed a multitude without food. **God does His best work where natural sufficiency ends.**

The lie of lack says you are limited. The truth of God says He is your limitless Source.

Recognizing lack as a lie—not your reality—is the first step toward walking in Kingdom abundance.

REFLECTION & DISCUSSION

1. When has the lie of lack stopped you from stepping out in faith?

2. What emotions or fears tend to surface when you feel you "don't have enough"?

3. How does Scripture challenge the idea that you must have everything you need before you obey God?

APPLICATION | ***ACTION STEPS***

Identify one area where you have been waiting for "enough" before moving forward.

Take one small step this week that reflects trust instead of fear—such as finishing a task, giving a compliment, or moving forward on something you've delayed.

RENEW YOUR MIND

Throughout the week, speak and meditate on this truth:

"Lack is a lie—God is my Source!"

Let this truth replace every fear of not having enough.

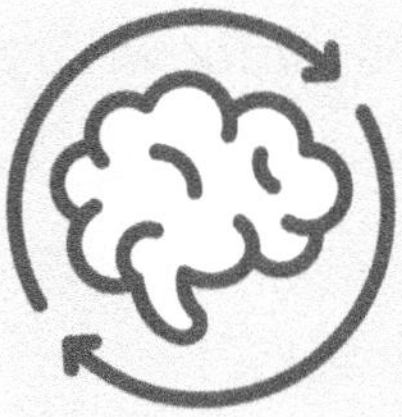

DECLARATION OF FAITH

"Lack is a lie, not my identity.
I refuse fear and embrace faith.
God is my Source, and He supplies more than enough
for everything He has called me to do."

Prayer

Father, thank You for exposing the lie of lack. Show me every place where this mindset has taken root in my heart. Replace it with faith, confidence, and trust in Your provision. Lead me to act boldly, knowing You are my Source and my sufficiency. In Jesus' Name, amen.

RENEWING THE MIND

WEEK 9

Prosperity begins on the inside long before it shows up on the outside.

Your financial life will never rise above the level of your thinking. That is why one of the most essential elements of biblical prosperity is **mind renewal**—aligning your thoughts with what God says instead of what the world or your circumstances say.

Ashley explains that many believers try to change their financial situation through effort, hustle, or willpower, but without renewed thinking, those changes rarely last. Scripture teaches that transformation comes through the renewing of the mind (Romans 12:2). In other words, **you don't prosper because you try harder—you prosper because you think differently.**

Renewing the mind means:

- Replacing old beliefs with God's truth
- Recognizing the source of negative or fearful thoughts
- Addressing internal limitations, not external obstacles
- Allowing God's Word to reshape your expectations
- Seeing yourself as blessed, capable, and supplied

Wrong thinking creates mental ceilings that create limitation:

- "I'll never get ahead."
- "I'm just not good with money."
- "There's never enough."
- "People like me don't prosper."

God's truth removes those ceilings and replaces them with confidence, wisdom, and expectation. Renewing your mind is not a one-time event—it's a continual process. But each renewed thought becomes a stepping stone toward the abundance God has already provided.

REFLECTION & DISCUSSION

1. What financial belief or thought pattern have you repeated for most of your life?

2. Does it align with Scripture? If not, what truth needs to replace it?

3. How do you see the connection between mindset and prosperity in your own life?

APPLICATION | ***ACTION STEPS***

Choose one limiting belief about money or provision that you want to change.

Then practice catching that thought at least once this week and intentionally replacing it with God's truth.

RENEW YOUR MIND

Throughout the week, speak and meditate on this truth:

"My mind is being renewed to God's way of thinking."

Return to this phrase as you align your thoughts with His Word.

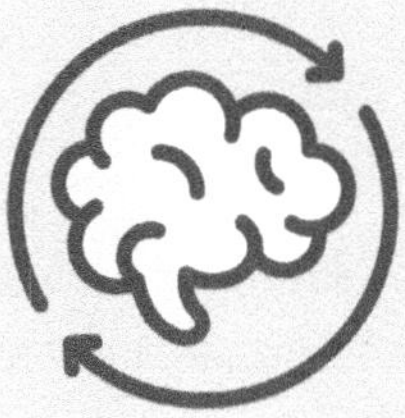

DECLARATION OF FAITH

"I renew my mind daily to God's Word.
I reject limiting beliefs and embrace truth.
My thinking aligns with God's provision,
and my life is being transformed from the inside out."

Prayer

Father, thank You for giving me the mind of Christ. Show me every belief that needs to change and every thought that doesn't line up with Your truth. Teach me to think in agreement with Your abundance, Your wisdom, and Your promises. I yield my mind to You, and I receive transformation. In Jesus' Name, amen.

TWO COMPETING SYSTEMS

WEEK 10

You can't live in God's Kingdom while thinking like the world.

Every believer must choose which system they will operate in: **the world's system** of scarcity, fear, and self-dependence, or **God's Kingdom system** of abundance, faith, and supernatural provision.

Ashley explains that these two systems are constantly at odds with each other. The world's system is driven by uncertainty, economic fluctuations, performance, and the belief that your future depends on your ability, effort, or connections. It teaches you to hold tightly, protect what you have, and expect shortage.

By contrast, God's system is rooted in His character. It operates by faith, not fear; obedience, not self-reliance; generosity, not hoarding; blessing, not toil. Kingdom economics is not subject to the world's instability because it flows from God's unchanging nature.

Throughout Scripture, God invites His people to live differently—to trust His provision even when circumstances look impossible. Whether it was manna in the wilderness, oil multiplying in a widow's home, or Jesus feeding thousands with a small lunch, God consistently demonstrates that **His system does not depend on earthly resources to function.**

Recognizing the existence of two competing systems helps you understand why many believers feel frustrated: They are trying to receive Kingdom promises while thinking in worldly patterns.

To walk in God's abundance, you must align your beliefs and decisions with His system—not the world's. The system you trust is the system you will experience.

REFLECTION & DISCUSSION

1. In what areas of your life do you feel most influenced by the world's system?

2. What stands out to you about how God's system operates differently from the world's?

3. What would it look like to fully trust God's system in your finances, decisions, or priorities?

APPLICATION | ***ACTION STEPS***

Write one area where you recognize the world's reasoning in your mind.

Rewrite that way of thinking through the lens of God's Kingdom system instead.

RENEW YOUR MIND

Throughout the week, speak and meditate on this truth:

"I choose God's system, and I refuse to bend to the pressure of the world's system."

Allow this to guide your decisions this week.

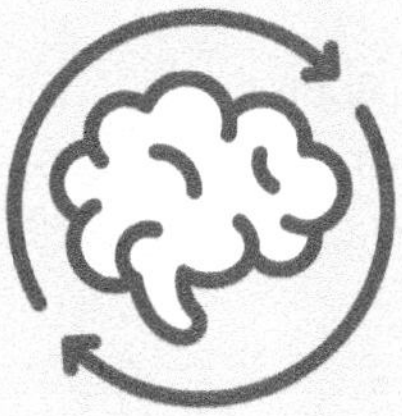

DECLARATION OF FAITH

"I recognize the two systems before me.
I reject the world's scarcity and choose God's abundance.
My decisions, thoughts, and expectations align with God's Kingdom.
I live by faith—not by fear."

Prayer

Father, thank You for inviting me into Your Kingdom system. Teach me to recognize the world's influence and to choose Your ways instead. Renew my thinking, strengthen my faith, and help me operate fully in Your abundance and wisdom. In Jesus' Name, amen.

THE SEED SYSTEM

WEEK 11

Everything in God's Kingdom grows from a seed.

God's Kingdom operates on a simple yet powerful principle: **increase begins with a seed.** From Genesis to the teachings of Jesus, the "seed system" is God's chosen way to produce growth, multiplication, and provision in the lives of His people.

Ashley explains that seedtime and harvest is not just a farming concept—it is a spiritual law woven into creation. Everything God does starts with a seed, whether it is an idea, a promise, a financial gift, an act of obedience, or a step of faith. God supplies seed, you sow it, and He brings the harvest.

This system also includes **stewardship**, because what you do with the seed determines its outcome. A seed left unsown cannot produce. A seed squandered cannot multiply. But a seed that is tended, stewarded, and placed in God's hands becomes a channel for supernatural increase.

The seed system teaches us:

- God provides the seed—not the world.
- You choose where to plant it.
- Growth is God's responsibility, not yours.
- Stewardship positions you for multiplication.
- The harvest always exceeds the seed.

This principle removes pressure from your shoulders. You don't have to make increase happen—you simply have to **sow faithfully and steward wisely**, trusting God to multiply what you give Him. The seed system empowers you to participate in God's abundance, not strive for it.

REFLECTION & DISCUSSION

1. What examples of God using "seeds" (ideas, actions, resources, etc.) can you identify in Scripture or in your own life?

2. How does understanding the seed system shift the way you view increase or financial breakthrough?

3. In what ways has God already given you seed to sow—time, finances, skills, opportunities, or acts of obedience?

APPLICATION | *ACTION STEPS*

Write down one seed you recognize in your life right now (time, finances, encouragement, skill, etc.).

Document how you sow that seed in some small, intentional way this week.

RENEW YOUR MIND

Throughout the week, speak and meditate on this truth:

"God multiplies the seeds I sow."

Let this shape your expectations as you recognize the seeds in your life.

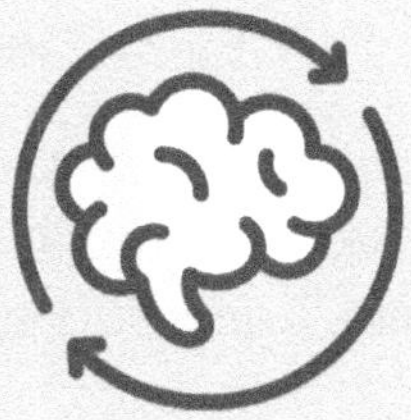

DECLARATION OF FAITH

"God has given me seed to sow, and I steward it with wisdom and faith.
I trust Him to multiply what I place in His hands.
Increase comes from the Lord, and I participate in
His abundance through the seeds I sow."

Prayer

Father, thank You for the seed You have placed in my life. Show me how to sow, where to sow, and how to steward well what You've entrusted to me. I trust You for the harvest and choose to participate in Your Kingdom system of increase. In Jesus' Name, amen.

SUPERNATURAL MULTIPLICATION

WEEK 12

God doesn't just add—He multiplies.

Supernatural multiplication is one of the most striking demonstrations of God's Kingdom system. Throughout Scripture, God doesn't merely replace what is lacking—He multiplies what is surrendered. Whether it was the widow's oil, the loaves and fishes, or the nets overflowing with fish, God consistently transforms small offerings into abundant supply.

Ashley explains that multiplication happens when:

- You give God something to work with
- You act in obedience rather than fear
- You expect increase rather than loss
- You refuse to limit God with natural thinking

The world's system says: "Hold on to what you have. You might lose it." But God's system says: "Place what you have in My hands and watch it multiply."

Supernatural multiplication requires a divine partnership. God performs the miracle, but you initiate it through faith—by sowing, giving, acting, and trusting. What you offer may look small, but nothing is small once it enters God's system. He specializes in taking what seems insignificant and producing more than enough!

The purpose of multiplication is not merely personal comfort. It's about equipping you to give more, bless more, reach more, and fulfill the assignments God has given you. Multiplication expands your capacity to make Kingdom impact. When you expect supernatural multiplication, you stop evaluating your future by what you currently possess. You begin to see what God can do with what's in your hands.

REFLECTION & DISCUSSION

1. What examples of supernatural multiplication in Scripture stand out to you most? Why?

2. Has God ever multiplied something in your life—resources, opportunities, relationships, or ideas?

3. What do you sense God is asking you to place in His hands to multiply?

APPLICATION | ***ACTION STEPS***

Write one area where you want to see God multiply what you surrender.

Then choose one small thing to release into God's hands—an idea, a task, a resource, or worry—and trust Him with it.

RENEW YOUR MIND

Throughout the week, speak and meditate on this truth:

"God multiplies what I surrender to Him."

Come back to this whenever you feel pressure to make things happen yourself.

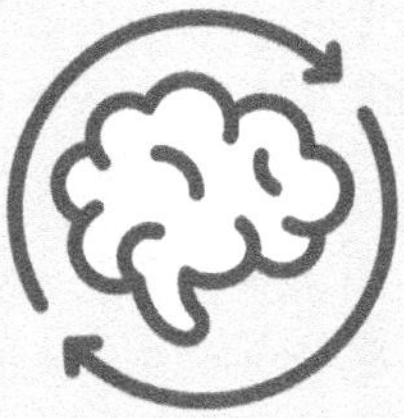

DECLARATION OF FAITH

"I trust God for supernatural multiplication.
I refuse to limit Him by natural reasoning.
What I place in His hands increases.
My life is a testimony of His abundant provision."

Prayer

Father, thank You for being the God of multiplication. Teach me to trust You with what I have, no matter how small it seems. Help me recognize opportunities for faith and obedience. Multiply the seeds I sow and the steps I take, for Your glory and Your Kingdom. In Jesus' Name, amen.

GRACE-BASED PROSPERITY

WEEK 13

Prosperity isn't earned—it's received.

Prosperity in the Kingdom of God is rooted in **grace**, not human effort. Many believers unknowingly approach finances with a performance mindset: "If I work harder, try harder, or become more spiritual, then maybe God will bless me." But Ashley explains that true biblical prosperity flows from the same place as salvation, healing, and righteousness: **the finished work of Jesus.**

Grace-based prosperity means:

- God blesses because He is good, not because you are perfect.
- Provision is part of your inheritance, not a reward.
- You don't earn prosperity—you receive it through faith.
- God's kindness, not your effort, is the foundation of increase.

Just as you cannot earn righteousness by good behavior, you cannot earn prosperity through striving. The moment you believe provision depends on your performance, you place yourself back under a system God freed you from. Grace shifts your posture:

- From striving → to resting
- From earning → to receiving
- From fear → to confidence
- From pressure → to trust

When you understand that prosperity is a gift of grace, you stop disqualifying yourself and begin expecting God's goodness to manifest. Faith simply receives what grace has already provided. This frees you from guilt around blessing, anxiety about finances, and the exhausting belief that everything depends on you. Grace-based prosperity empowers you to live in the flow of God's provision with peace, joy, and confidence.

REFLECTION & DISCUSSION

1. Have you ever felt that God's provision depended on your performance? In what ways?

2. How does seeing prosperity as part of grace reshape your expectations?

3. What would change in your mindset if you believed you were already qualified for abundance?

APPLICATION | ***ACTION STEPS***

Write down one way you have tried to "earn" God's provision.

Then intentionally receive His grace in that area this week by thanking Him for providing apart from your performance. Write out your thanksgiving!

RENEW YOUR MIND

Throughout the week, speak and meditate on this truth:

"Prosperity is a gift of grace, and I receive it by faith."

Let this truth dismantle any sense of unworthiness or need to strive to earn God's provision.

DECLARATION OF FAITH

"God's prosperity is mine by grace, not by works.
I stop striving and start receiving.
I am qualified for abundance because of Jesus,
and I walk in His provision with confidence and peace."

Prayer

Father, thank You that prosperity is part of the grace You freely give. Show me every place where I've tried to earn what You meant for me to receive. Teach me to rest, trust, and believe Your Word. Help me walk boldly in everything Jesus provided for me. In His Name, amen.

FAITH FOR FINANCES

WEEK 14

Faith receives what grace has already provided.

If prosperity is provided by grace, then **faith** is how you take hold of it. Ashley explains that many Christians believe God can provide, but they struggle to believe He *will*—for them, personally, consistently, and abundantly. This gap between knowing and receiving is where faith becomes essential.

Faith for finances is no different than faith for salvation or healing. It comes from hearing the Word, agreeing with it, and acting on it. Faith does not try to convince God to move; rather, it rests in what God has already done. Faith does not beg—it receives!

Faith for finances means:

- Believing God is your Source
- Trusting Him above circumstances
- Acting in obedience even when you don't see the outcome
- Speaking what He says instead of what fear says
- Expecting His provision, not just hoping for it

The world's system teaches you to rely on logic, effort, and security. But God invites you to rely on Him. Financial faith grows as you see Him as Provider, as you meditate on His promises, and as you take small steps of trust.

Fear says, "What if I don't have enough?" **Faith says**, "God supplies all my needs according to His riches." **Fear waits** for stability before obeying. **Faith obeys** and watches stability follow.

Faith for finances is not about forcing an outcome—it is about aligning your heart with God's truth so you can confidently receive His provision.

REFLECTION & DISCUSSION

1. In what areas of your finances do you find it hardest to trust God?

2. What promises from Scripture strengthen your faith for provision?

3. What step of faith—big or small—do you sense God inviting you to take?

APPLICATION | *ACTION STEPS*

Write one financial situation you have been worrying about.

This week, take one faith-filled action—such as speaking a scripture, making a decision, or releasing anxiety to God.

RENEW YOUR MIND

Throughout the week, speak and meditate on this truth:

"I trust God with my finances, and I receive His provision by faith."

Use this phrase to quiet fear and strengthen your confidence in God.

DECLARATION OF FAITH

"I walk by faith in every area of my life—including my finances.
I trust God as my Source.
I speak His promises, believe His Word,
and receive His provision with confidence."

Prayer

Father, thank You for teaching me to trust You with my finances. Strengthen my faith as I meditate on Your Word. Help me step out in obedience, think with confidence, and receive everything You have already provided for me in Christ. I choose faith over fear. In Jesus' Name, amen.

REMOVING UNBELIEF

WEEK 15

Faith grows when unbelief is removed.

Unbelief is often the hidden barrier that prevents believers from experiencing God's provision. It is not the absence of faith—it's the presence of competing thoughts that contradict God's Word. Ashley explains that you can have genuine faith in one area and unbelief in another, and the unbelief will short-circuit your ability to receive.

Unbelief sounds like:

- "Maybe God doesn't want to provide for me."
- "What if it doesn't work this time?"
- "I know God can... but will He for me?"
- "My situation is too far gone."

These aren't just doubts—they are deeply rooted beliefs formed by past experiences, disappointments, or fear. The goal is not to "try harder" to believe, but to **identify and remove the thoughts that oppose God's promises**.

Jesus showed that unbelief, not a lack of God's power, limits breakthrough. When the disciples couldn't cast out a demon, He didn't say they needed more faith—He said they needed less unbelief. Removing unbelief happens by:

- Renewing your mind with truth and Exchanging lies for Scripture
- Guarding your thoughts and Meditating on God's goodness
- Speaking faith instead of fear and Refusing to rehearse worst-case scenarios

When unbelief is removed, even small faith becomes powerful. You stop questioning God's willingness and start expecting His goodness. You stop hesitating and begin receiving! Removing unbelief clears the channel so grace can flow freely.

REFLECTION & DISCUSSION

1. What fearful or limiting thoughts tend to rise up when you think about finances?

2. Can you identify a belief you've held that contradicts God's promises?

3. What truth from Scripture directly challenges that unbelief?

APPLICATION | *ACTION STEPS*

Write down one lie or limiting belief that has influenced your financial thinking.

Actively refuse it this week by writing down the truth that refutes it. What is one small step you can take to put action to this faith?

RENEW YOUR MIND

Throughout the week, speak and meditate on this truth:

"I remove unbelief and receive God's truth."

Let this guide your thoughts whenever doubts attempt to rise.

DECLARATION OF FAITH

"I refuse every thought that contradicts God's promises.
Unbelief has no place in my heart.
I meditate on truth, speak truth,
and receive everything God has provided through grace."

Prayer

Father, thank You for exposing every belief that has held me back. Show me where unbelief has taken root, and help me replace it with Your truth. Renew my mind, strengthen my faith, and help me walk boldly in Your provision. In Jesus' Name, amen.

ROLE OF DILIGENCE

WEEK 16

God blesses the work of your hands, not the wishes of your heart.

While prosperity begins with grace and is received through faith, it is **expressed through diligence**. Ashley explains that diligence is not striving, pressure, or endless busyness—it is the intentional, consistent application of effort that aligns with God's wisdom and purpose.

Diligence is not the source of prosperity; God is. But diligence is often the **vehicle** through which prosperity flows. Scripture consistently highlights the value of diligence:

- *"The hand of the diligent makes rich."* – Proverbs 10:4, NKJV
- *"Whatever your hand finds to do, do it with your might."* – Ecclesiastes 9:10, NKJV
- *"A faithful man will abound with blessings."* – Proverbs 28:20, NKJV

Diligence is not about overworking—it is about stewardship. It means showing up, being faithful, taking responsibility, and applying excellence to whatever God places in your hands. A diligent heart says:

- "I will do my part, and trust God with the outcome."
- "I will be faithful in little so I can be entrusted with more."
- "I will align my actions with my faith."

Many believers wait for financial breakthrough without taking the practical steps that allow increase to take root. Diligence prepares the soil. It positions you for opportunity, multiplies what you have, and partners with the Holy Spirit to produce real fruit.

Diligence does not replace faith; it **expresses** faith. It shows God you are ready for the increase He desires to bring.

REFLECTION & DISCUSSION

1. How has your view of diligence changed as you've grown in understanding biblical prosperity?

2. What are some practical ways you can show diligence in this season of your life?

3. Do you tend to overwork or underwork? What motivates that pattern?

APPLICATION | ***ACTION STEPS***

Choose one area where you'd like to grow in diligence.

Take one simple step toward it this week. For example, organize something, finish a task, or set aside time to focus.

RENEW YOUR MIND

Throughout the week, speak and meditate on this truth:

"God blesses the work of my hands."

Allow this truth to motivate and encourage your diligence.

DECLARATION OF FAITH

"I am diligent, faithful, and committed to what God has entrusted to me.
My actions align with my faith,
and God blesses the work of my hands.
I am prepared, positioned, and ready for increase."

Prayer

Father, thank You for giving me the ability and wisdom to work with diligence. Show me where to focus my efforts and how to steward well what You've placed in my hands. Strengthen my consistency and guide my steps. I trust You to bless the work I do in faith. In Jesus' Name, amen.

EXCELLENCE & WORK HABITS

WEEK 17

Excellence is not perfection. It is stewardship that honors God.

Excellence is a Kingdom principle. It is not about impressing people or achieving flawlessness—it's about **honoring God with the way you approach what He has entrusted to you**. Ashley teaches that excellence positions you for increase because it reflects a heart that takes responsibility, values stewardship, and operates with intentionality.

Excellence says:

- "I will do my best with what I have."
- "I will work as unto the Lord" (Colossians 3:23).
- "I will treat small opportunities as preparation for greater ones."

Work habits rooted in excellence reveal faith in action. Poor habits—procrastination, sloppiness, inconsistency, or passivity—don't necessarily mean a lack of desire; they often mean a lack of alignment. When your work habits align with God's wisdom, your life becomes fertile ground for opportunity and increase. Excellence is not striving. It is willingness to learn, grow, improve, and show up with your whole heart.

Throughout Scripture, God entrusted more to those who were faithful with what they already had. Jesus taught that those who are faithful in little will be given much. Excellence attracts increase because it demonstrates readiness! God is not looking for perfection—He is looking for faithfulness expressed through effort, attitude, and consistency.

REFLECTION & DISCUSSION

1. How would you describe your current work habits—steady, inconsistent, distracted, diligent, or something else?

2. What does "excellence" mean to you in the context of your work, calling, or daily responsibilities?

3. What small, consistent change could you make in your habits that would honor God and strengthen your stewardship?

APPLICATION | ***ACTION STEPS***

Choose one area where you want to elevate your level of excellence—for example, your workspace, schedule, responsibilities, giving, planning, or communication.

Practice excellence in one small, specific moment this week. Write down what you did and how it made you feel.

RENEW YOUR MIND

Throughout the week, speak and meditate on this truth:

"I pursue excellence as an act of worship."

Let this shape your attitude toward each task you take on.

DECLARATION OF FAITH

"I am committed to excellence in what God has placed in my hands.
My work habits reflect His wisdom and character.
I steward opportunities well, prepare faithfully,
and attract increase through faithfulness."

Prayer

Father, thank You for entrusting me with gifts, opportunities, and responsibilities. Teach me to walk in excellence and develop habits that honor You. Help me remove distractions, grow in consistency, and approach every task with faithfulness and purpose. In Jesus' Name, amen.

DILIGENCE WITHOUT STRIVING

WEEK 18

Work with God, not for God.

Diligence is a Kingdom virtue—but striving is not. Ashley explains that many believers swing between two unhealthy extremes: **passivity**, where nothing moves forward, and **striving**, where everything depends on human effort. Biblical diligence lives in the healthy middle: faith-filled action led by the Holy Spirit.

Striving says:

- "It all depends on me."
- "If I don't make this happen, nothing will."
- "I have to earn God's blessing."

Passivity says:

- "God will do everything; I don't need to participate."
- "I'm waiting for conditions to be perfect."
- "I'll move when I feel motivated."

But diligence—**true, Spirit-led diligence**—says:

- "I will do my part, and trust God with the results."
- "I will act in obedience, not pressure."
- "I will work from rest, not *for* rest."

Jesus modeled this balance beautifully. He worked intentionally, consistently, and purposefully—but never anxiously. He said, *"My Father has been working until now, and I have been working."* His diligence flowed from relationship, not performance.

Striving wears you out. **Passivity** holds you back. But **diligence**, partnered with **grace**, produces fruit.

REFLECTION & DISCUSSION

1. Which extreme do you tend to fall into more often—passivity or striving? Why?

2. What does "working with God" look like in the season you're in right now?

3. How would your life change if you replaced pressure-driven effort with Spirit-led diligence?

APPLICATION | ***ACTION STEPS***

Identify one area where you've been striving, or one area where you've been passive.

Then take one balanced action—neither pressured nor passive—that reflects working with God.

RENEW YOUR MIND

Throughout the week, speak and meditate on this truth:

"I am diligent, not driven. I work *with* God, not apart from Him."

Return to this phrase whenever you feel pressure or passivity pulling at you.

DECLARATION OF FAITH

"I refuse both passivity and striving.
I choose diligence that flows from grace.
God leads my steps, strengthens my hands,
and blesses the work I do in partnership with Him."

Prayer

Father, thank You for teaching me the difference between striving and diligence. Help me walk in balance—faithful, consistent, and Spirit-led. Remove the pressure to perform, and replace it with confidence that You are working in and through me. I commit my efforts to You and trust You with the results. In Jesus' Name, amen.

GIVING AS FAITH

WEEK 19

Giving isn't losing—it's trusting.

Giving is one of the clearest expressions of faith in the life of a believer. Ashley explains that when you give, you are making a bold declaration: **"God is my Source, and I trust Him."**

It shifts your confidence away from your own ability and onto God's provision.

In the world's system, giving seems risky—something that decreases what you have. But in God's Kingdom, giving initiates increase. Scripture teaches:

- *"Give, and it will be given to you."* – Luke 6:38
- *"He who sows bountifully will also reap bountifully."* – 2 Corinthians 9:6
- *"There is one who scatters, yet increases more."* – Proverbs 11:24

Giving as faith means:

- You give because you **trust God**, not because you have extra.
- You give as a **response to grace**, not obligation.
- You give to participate in **God's system**, not the world's.
- You give **expecting** God to **multiply** seed sown, not reduce your supply.

Fear of giving comes from the lie of lack. Confidence in giving comes from seeing God as Provider. When you give, you release your seed into God's hands—and He treats every seed as the beginning of a harvest.

Giving is not about money leaving your life; it's about putting that money into a higher, supernatural system where it can bear fruit. **Giving is faith in motion.**

REFLECTION & DISCUSSION

1. What emotions come up for you when you think about giving generously?

2. How does seeing giving as an act of faith—rather than obligation—change your perspective?

3. Has God ever used giving to stretch your faith or reveal His provision?

APPLICATION | ***ACTION STEPS***

Identify an area where God may be prompting you to give—finances, time, encouragement, resources, or support.

Then look for an opportunity to give in any form this week—time, kindness, prayer, or finances—as an act of faith.

RENEW YOUR MIND

Throughout the week, speak and meditate on this truth:

"My giving is an act of faith, and God supplies my seed."

Let this truth bring confidence and joy to your giving!

DECLARATION OF FAITH

"I give boldly, cheerfully, and in faith.
God is my Source, and I trust His provision.
My giving opens the door to increase,
and my seed produces a harvest in God's Kingdom."

Prayer

Father, thank You for allowing me to participate in Your Kingdom through giving. Teach me to give in faith, without fear or hesitation. Show me where to sow, how to obey, and how to trust You fully with my resources. Multiply every seed I sow for Your glory. In Jesus' Name, amen.

TYPES OF GIVING

WEEK 20

Different seeds produce different harvests.

Not all giving is the same. Scripture reveals multiple types of giving, each with a unique purpose, heart posture, and harvest attached to it. Ashley explains that understanding these distinctions helps you give with intention and faith instead of habit or obligation.

Some types of giving found in Scripture include:

1. Tithes – Honor
   The tithe acknowledges God as your Source. It is an act of worship, not payment. Tithing places your finances under God's care and aligns your heart with His provision.
2. Offerings – Generosity
   Offerings go beyond the tithe and reflect a heart of abundance. They are the overflow of gratitude and a response to the prompting of the Holy Spirit.
3. Alms – Compassion
   Giving to the poor is close to God's heart. Proverbs says that when you give to the poor, you "lend to the Lord." This type of giving produces a harvest of mercy, protection, and favor.
4. Seed Giving – Increase
   This is intentional, faith-filled sowing for a specific harvest. It is not manipulation or transaction—it is participation in the spiritual law of sowing and reaping.

Each type of giving is meaningful, but they produce different effects. Understanding these differences empowers you to sow with clarity and expectation. What you sow determines what you reap—financially, spiritually, and relationally. Giving with purpose deepens your faith and multiplies your impact!

REFLECTION & DISCUSSION

1. Which form of giving feels the most natural to you? Which one challenges you the most?

2. How has your understanding of tithes, offerings, alms, or seed giving changed over time?

3. What type of giving do you feel God is inviting you to grow in?

APPLICATION | ***ACTION STEPS***

Write down one type of giving (tithe, offering, alms, seed) that you want to grow in.

Take one simple step in that area this week—whatever fits your faith and season.

RENEW YOUR MIND

Throughout the week, speak and meditate on this truth:

"My giving is purposeful, powerful, and led by the Holy Spirit."

Allow this truth to direct your generosity with clarity and faith.

DECLARATION OF FAITH

"I give with purpose and understanding.
I honor God with my tithe, sow seeds with faith,
show compassion through alms,
and give offerings from a heart of abundance.
God multiplies every seed I sow."

Prayer

Father, thank You for teaching me the power and purpose of giving. Show me where and how to give with intention. Lead me by Your Spirit, fill me with generosity, and bless every seed I sow according to Your Word. In Jesus' Name, amen.

LIFESTYLE OF GENEROSITY

WEEK 21

Generosity isn't an act. it's a way of living.

Generosity is the culmination of everything you've learned throughout this study. Ashley explains that biblical prosperity isn't complete until it overflows. God doesn't bless you simply to improve your personal comfort—He blesses you so you can participate in His purposes, advance His Kingdom, and reveal His heart to the world.

A lifestyle of generosity is marked by:

1. A willing heart
   Generosity is not driven by pressure or obligation. It is rooted in joy, gratitude, and trust in God's provision.
2. Sensitivity to the Holy Spirit
   Generous people listen. They are open to God's nudges—give here, help there, encourage this person, sow into that ministry.
3. Consistent giving
   Generosity is not occasional; it becomes a natural rhythm. You give because it's who you are, not because someone asked.
4. Kingdom perspective
   You see your resources as tools for impact, not just personal use. Money becomes a servant, not a master.

Living generously reflects God's nature. You are never more like your Father than when you give—He loved, so He gave. Generosity moves you from simply "having enough" to becoming a channel of blessing to others. And as you pour out, God continually replenishes your supply.

Prosperity begins with grace, grows through faith, expresses itself in diligence, and culminates in a generous, overflowing life.

REFLECTION & DISCUSSION

1. How has your view of generosity changed during this study?

2. What does a "lifestyle of generosity" look like for you personally?

3. Who or what has God placed on your heart to bless, help, or encourage?

APPLICATION | ***ACTION STEPS***

Write one way you want generosity to show up in your lifestyle moving forward.

Intentionally practice generosity once this week in a way that reflects who you are becoming. Document here what you did.

RENEW YOUR MIND

Throughout the week, speak and meditate on this truth:

"I am blessed to be a blessing!"

Let this confession shape your identity and your overflow.

DECLARATION OF FAITH

"I live generously because God has been generous to me.
I am a giver, a sower, and a channel of blessing.
My life overflows with the goodness of God,
and through generosity, I impact the world for His glory."

Prayer

Father, thank You for leading me into a generous life. Fill my heart with Your love and compassion. Show me opportunities to give, to help, to sow, and to bless. Make my life an open channel of Your goodness, and may everything I give reflect Your abundant grace. In Jesus' Name, amen.

CONCLUSION

Prosperity is not a destination. it's a continuous relationship lived out with God every day.

Over the last 21 weeks, you have walked through a journey of truth, renewal, and transformation. You've seen that God is a good Father. You've discovered that prosperity comes by grace, is received through faith, grows through diligence, and overflows in generosity. You've confronted old beliefs, embraced new truths, and stepped into the reality that **God wants you rich: spirit, soul, and body.**

But this is not the end of your journey. It is the beginning of a new way of living!

Prosperity is not measured only in dollars or material resources. It is revealed in peace, confidence, influence, generosity, and intimacy with God. It is expressed in the way you think, speak, work, give, and walk out your purpose. As you continue growing, the Holy Spirit will keep leading you into deeper understanding and new opportunities to apply everything you've learned.

You have been equipped with biblical principles that work in every season and circumstance. Whether you are facing increase or challenge, abundance or transition, the truths in this study remain solid and unchanging. **God is your Source. His grace is sufficient. His promises are sure.** And He delights in your success even more than you do!

MOVING FORWARD

As you continue your walk with God:

- Keep renewing your mind to His goodness.
- Keep acting in faith, not fear.
- Keep stewarding what He places in your hands.
- Keep giving generously and joyfully.
- Keep expecting God to multiply your seed.
- Keep living with vision, purpose, and confidence.

You are not the same person who started this study! You have new understanding, new expectancy, and new boldness. And God is not finished—He is only getting started.

FINAL DECLARATION

"I am blessed, favored, and equipped.
God is my Source, and I trust His provision.
I walk in abundance, stewardship, generosity, and purpose.
My life reflects the goodness of God,
and I am empowered to prosper in every area."

Closing Prayer

Father, thank You for everything You have revealed during this journey. Seal these truths in my heart. Help me walk in Your wisdom, Your favor, and Your abundance every day. Lead me by Your Spirit, strengthen my faith, and guide my steps. May my life display Your goodness, and may every blessing You entrust to me become a blessing to others. I step forward in confidence, knowing You are my Provider, my Shepherd, and my Source. In Jesus' Name, amen.

FREE
CONFESSION
CARD

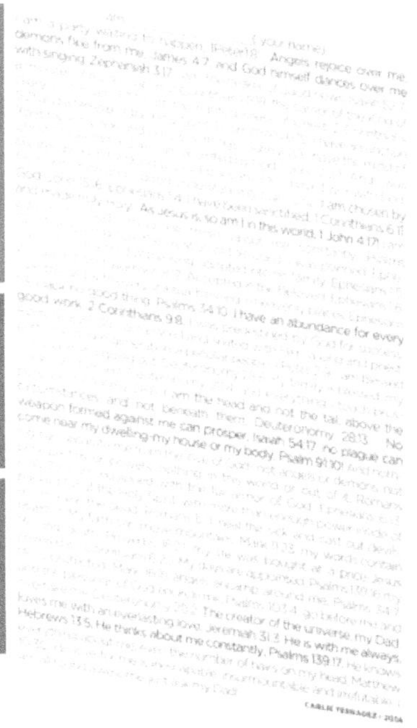

WHO DO YOU THINK YOU ARE?

The partners of Terradez Ministries have made it possible for us to provide this gift to you! The most powerful scriptures from God's Word, declaring who you are in Christ, can all be found in one place; the Terradez Ministries' Confession Card! In this colorful, fun, "prescription-sized" confession card, you will speak out your true identity in Christ daily! As you speak God's Word over yourself it will soon become a living reality.

discover your
TRUE IDENTITY
today!

SCAN ME

OTHER BOOKS
BY TERRADEZ MINISTRIES

God Wants You Rich: *The Scandalous Truth*

God Wants You Rich reveals God's perspective on wealth, correcting misconceptions about prosperity, showing money as a tool for His glory, and encouraging believers to embrace abundance, freedom, and blessing through biblical understanding.

Exposing the Spirit of Mammon
Make God, not money, your master!

Exposing the Spirit of Mammon reveals the deceptive spirit of mammon, teaching readers to reject money as master, recognize manipulation, hear God's voice, gain financial freedom, and walk in God's blessing today always.

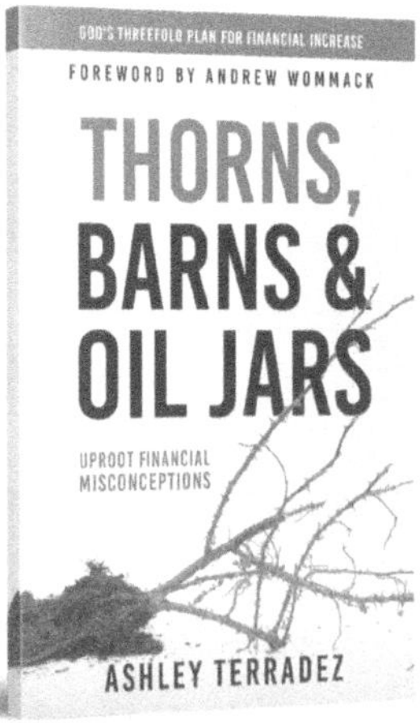

Thorns, Barns & Oil Jars:
Uproot Financial Misconceptions

Thorns, Barns & Oil Jars corrects unbiblical financial beliefs, teaches biblical principles for provision, saving, and increase, and empowers readers with practical guidance and testimonies to experience prosperity, freedom and alignment with God's plan.

AVAILABLE ON OUR WEBSITE
TERRADEZ.COM/SHOP

EMPOWERING BELIEVERS
IN THE PROMISES OF GOD

Ashley and Carlie Terradez are a power-packed duo, exercising Luke 4:18 by proclaiming and providing an example of God's promises and provision through Christ Jesus. With a special emphasis on relationship with God, supernatural healing, and financial provision, we empower people to access everything that Jesus has already provided for us through His death, burial, and resurrection.

On our website, you will find many free ministry resources and discipleship programs made available by our generous partners.

TerradezMinistries.com

Connect with Us

Terradez Ministries
Terradez Ministries
@terradezministries
TerradezMinistries.com
info@terradez.com
+1 (719) 600-3344
6660 Delmonico Dr. Suite D272,
Colorado Springs, CO 80919

SCAN ME

Made in United States
Cleveland, OH
05 November 2026

47669898R00030